SELECTIONS FROM THE PSALMS

A LIFE OF WORSHIP

Other studies in the Not Your Average Bible Study series

Ruth

Jonah

Malachi

Sermon on the Mount

Ephesians

Colossians

Hebrews

James

1 Peter

2 Peter and Jude

1–3 John

For updates on this series, visit lexhampress.com/nyab

SELECTIONS FROM THE
PSALMS
A LIFE OF WORSHIP

NOT YOUR AVERAGE BIBLE STUDY

MILES CUSTIS

Selections from the Psalms: A Life of Worship
Not Your Average Bible Study

Copyright 2014 Lexham Press
Adapted with permission from content originally published in *Bible Study Magazine* (Issues 5.3–5.4)

Lexham Press, 1313 Commercial St., Bellingham, WA 98225
LexhamPress.com

ISBN: 978-1-57-799553-1

Editor-in-Chief: John D. Barry
Managing Editor: Rebecca Van Noord
Assistant Editors: Jessi Strong, Elizabeth Vince, Joel Wilcox
Cover Design: Christine Gerhart
Typesetting: projectluz.com

CONTENTS

HOW TO USE
THIS RESOURCE

Not Your Average Bible Study is a series of in-depth Bible studies that can be used for individual or group study. Depending on your individual needs or your group pace, you may opt to cover one lesson a week or more.

Each lesson prompts you to dig deep into the Word—as such, we recommend you use your preferred translation with this study. The author used his own translation, but included quotations from the English Standard Version. Whatever Bible version you use, please be sure you leave ample time to get into the Bible itself.

To assist you, we recommend using the Faithlife Study Bible, which contains notes written by Miles Custis and is also edited by John D. Barry. You can download this digital resource for free for your tablet, phone, personal computer, or use it online. Go to FaithlifeBible.com to learn more.

May God bless you in the study of His Word.

INTRODUCTION

When our hearts are filled with joy, its easy to approach God to offer Him praise and thanks. But when we face pain or sorrow, we often choose to sort out such emotions on our own. Worship is typically the last thing on our mind when we feel abandoned or in despair.

Yet in the Psalms, the Israelites boldly cry out to God in all circusmtances and with all emotions—peace and turmoil, joy and sorrow, faith and confusion. The Psalms provide us with a model for approaching God in authentic worship no matter our situation. They demonstrate the great intimacy we can have with the Father who desires to hear from us at all times, as He continually draws us closer to Him.

PART I

A SPECTRUM OF PRAISE

We often think of worship as joyful noises and hands lifted in praise. Expressions of grief, frustration and fear don't fit the mold of worship— they're often sorted out privately.

The Psalms challenge our modern constructs about emotions. They give voice to the joyful and desperate cries of an ancient people in a manner that many of us would hesitate to express today. The Psalms abandon façades, choosing complete authenticity before God. They certainly express praise with songs that recount God's creative work and His acts throughout history (e.g., Pss 104–106), but they also capture the raw and almost hostile cries of people who struggle to understand God's work. Lament psalms question God's reasons for perceived abandonment (such as "Why have you forsaken me?" in Psa 22:1). Some psalms reveal people's feelings about their faith struggles, as they question why the wicked prosper, or wrestle with the reality of exile (e.g., Pss 73, 137).

The Psalms show us the great intimacy we have with God though our words of expression, from songs of praise to cries of desperation accompanied by demands that God take action. Because they were part of Israel's worship, the Psalms also illustrate how open and honest we can be. No matter what situation we are facing, the turmoil, joy or confusion we experience as a result can be brought to Him. In these eight lessons, we'll examine eight different types of psalms and what they reveal about how we worship and relate to God.

PRAISE THE LORD

Pray that God would give you a spirit of praise toward Him.

Read Psalm 146.

Psalm 146 is a praise psalm. The psalmist leads worshipers by encouraging them to "Praise the Lord." The well-known Hebrew phrase "Hallelujah" opens and closes the psalm. This phrase isn't just an offering of praise—it is a command directed at God's people that they "Praise the Lord." What does "praise" mean to you? In what ways and situations do you praise God? How are you neglecting to do so?

_____

_____

_____

The psalmist speaks about trusting in princes (146:3–4). Why would the psalmist warn against putting your trust in another person? Who should we trust instead?

_____

_____

_____

Compare Psalm 20:7. Have there been times when you put your trust in people (including yourself) rather than God? What actions can you take to trust God fully?

_____

_____

_____

Psalm 146:5 says that those who put their hope in the Lord are "blessed." Write down all the ways the psalmist describes God (146:6–7). What aspects of this description give you the most confidence about your hope in God?

_____

_____

_____

How does God's role as creator contrast with the "princes" of 146:3–4?

_____

_____

_____

The psalmist praises the actions of the Lord (146:7–9). What type of people does God help? Which of these groups do you relate to? How do these actions reflect God's character? How does God's concern for the downtrodden encourage you to praise Him?

_____

_____

_____

For more praise psalms, read Psalms 8, 103, 111 and 148. Which aspects of God's character do these psalms emphasize? How are these psalms different? How are they similar? How do they encourage you to praise God?

_____

_____

_____

BE GRACIOUS TO ME

Pray that God would sustain you by His steadfast love.

Read Psalm 6.

Psalm 6 is an individual lament psalm. These types of psalms display raw honesty as the psalmists often complain to God. These complaints rise out of suffering due to external forces (like enemies or oppressors) or internal forces (like sickness or physical suffering).

Here, the psalmist pleads with God to deliver him. He first begs that God not discipline him in anger. In the Bible, God's discipline is usually portrayed as a positive means of receiving instruction (see Prov 3:11–12). Have you ever felt like God was disciplining you? Why does the psalmist ask God here not to rebuke or discipline him? (Compare Jer 10:24.)

_____

_____

_____

_____

The psalmist describes his weakened state (Psa 6:2–7). His desperation is apparent in his cries for God to be gracious to him. Have you experienced physical or emotional desperation? How did you respond? Were you able to see God's hand in the situation and call to Him from your pain?

_____

_____

_____

_____

What does the psalmist appeal to when he asks God to save him (6:4)? How would saving the psalmist benefit God's "steadfast love"?

_____

_____

_____

What are some features of God's steadfast love that explain why the psalmist appeals to it? (Compare Psa 130:7–8 and Neh 1:5.) How have you seen God's steadfast love in your life?

_____

_____

_____

The psalmist ends by acknowledging God has heard him (Psa 6:9). Lament psalms often end with notes of praise that demonstrate the lamenters' confidence that God will rescue them. When you struggle, are you confident in God's help? How can the psalmist's example encourage you when your confidence wanes?

_____

_____

_____

For other individual lament psalms, read Psalms 10, 13, 38 and 142. How do the writers of these psalms address God? How can these psalms be an encouragement to you during difficult times?

_____

_____

_____

HAVE YOU FORGOTTEN US?

Pray that God would protect and grow His Church.

Read Psalm 44.

Psalm 44 is a corporate (group) lament psalm that would likely have been recited after a military defeat. As the community struggles to cope with a defeat in battle, the psalmist reminds God of the deeds that He performed for their ancestors (44:1–3). How would these accounts have influenced the people's trust in God? How do they influence your trust in God?

_____

_____

_____

What past events in your own life remind you of God's goodness during times of struggle?

_____

_____

_____

The psalmist asserts that the community has trusted in God (44:4–8). Despite this, it seems that God has rejected them (44:9–16). Why would the psalmist attribute their defeat to God rejecting them?

_____

_____

_____

_____

Have you ever felt like God has abandoned you? How can the psalmist's strong language, directed toward God, encourage you during trials?

_____

_____

_____

The psalmist repeats his assertion that the people have not forgotten God (44:17-22). Despite their faithfulness, they are suffering (44:19, 22). Why do you think the psalmist emphasizes the people's faithfulness? What is the relationship between the people's "boast" in God (44:8) and their suffering "for [His] sake" (44:22)? When you feel abandoned by God, do you honestly express that to Him?

_____

_____

_____

At the conclusion of the psalm, the psalmist calls for God to "wake up" and help His people (44:23-26). His language is surprisingly blunt. Have you ever addressed God in this way? How does a reminder of God's past deeds shed insight on these cries for help (44:1-3)? What great act of God reminds you of His love and faithfulness?

_____

_____

_____

For other corporate lament psalms, read Psalms 12, 74, 80 and 90. How do these psalms cry out to God? How can these psalms encourage you to honestly express your feelings to God?

_____

_____

_____

WHY SHOULD I FEAR?

Pray for the wisdom of God.

Read Psalm 49.

Psalm 49 is a wisdom psalm in which the psalmist invites all people to hear wisdom (49:1-4). Wisdom psalms focus on teaching or instruction rather than praise or worship. However, wisdom in the Old Testament has a moral aspect; it is closely related to fearing or trusting in God (see Psa 111:10; Prov 1:7; 15:33; Job 28:28). How would you describe the relationship between wisdom and fearing God? Can someone be wise without fearing God? Why or why not?

_____

_____

_____

The psalmist talks about not fearing the wickedness of those who trust in their wealth (Psa 49:5-6). What reasons does he give (49:7-9)? Why would he fear the iniquity of the wealthy? How can you apply this to a modern context?

_____

_____

_____

In Psalm 49:10-12, the psalmist discusses how all people—wise or foolish—will die. What point is he making with this observation? Is this thought encouraging?

_____

_____

_____

The book of Ecclesiastes makes a similar observation about death. Read Ecclesiastes 2:12–21. What point does that passage make about humanity's shared fate? How is this different than the point made in Psalm 49 (compare Eccl 2:18–21 with Psa 49:16–17)?

_____

_____

_____

How does the psalmist contrast the upright with those who have foolish confidence (49:13–15)? How does he portray an eternal perspective (49:16–20)? How does this encourage you during temporary struggles? In what ways can 49:15 be understood as a response to 49:5–6?

_____

_____

_____

For other wisdom psalms, read Psalms 14, 37, 73 and 112. What lessons can you take from these psalms? What are some tangible steps you can take to incorporate these teachings into your life?

_____

_____

_____

LET THEM BE PUT TO SHAME

Pray that the Spirit would help you understand God's righteousness.

Read Psalm 83.

Psalm 83 is an imprecatory psalm—the psalmist calls for God to judge his enemies. The psalmist begins by asking God not to be silent. What would cause the psalmist to think God was silent?

_____

_____

_____

Have you ever felt like God was not acting or offering direction when you wanted Him to? How did you respond? What did you learn through that situation?

_____

_____

_____

The psalmist describes how Israel's enemies are conspiring against them (83:2–8). How does he describe these enemies and their intentions? Have you ever felt like you were surrounded by people who oppressed you? How did you respond?

_____

_____

_____

_____

In the second half of the psalm, the psalmist calls for God to destroy his enemies (83:9–18). Passages like this are difficult to reconcile with verses like Matthew 5:43–44 that say "Love your enemies." Nations in the ancient Near East were closely associated with a particular deity. For Israel, defeating a nation was equivalent to defeating their god (compare 2 Kgs 19:10–19). Victory would show other nations that the Lord was truly God (note the reason the psalmist gives for God to destroy his enemies in Psa 83:16, 18).

Today, God has displayed victory over sin and death through Christ's death and resurrection (1 Cor 15:56). In light of Christ's victory, how can you lovingly help your "enemies" recognize God?

_____

_____

_____

For other imprecatory psalms, read Psalms 58, 69, 109 and 137. What do these psalms teach us about God's attitude toward evil and righteousness?

_____

_____

_____

THE LORD SAVES HIS ANOINTED

Pray that God would give you a confident trust in Him.

Read Psalm 20.

Psalm 20 is a royal psalm, one addressed to the king. The psalm may have been publicly recited as the king prepared to lead an army to battle. The psalmist hopes for God's protection and blessing on the king. How does the psalmist describe God's help (20:1–3)? Have you experienced God answering you in a "day of trouble"?

_____

_____

_____

_____

_____

What is the relationship between God's help and the offerings and sacrifices mentioned in 20:3? How does Christ's sacrificial and ongoing work assure us that we have help in our troubles (see Heb 4:14–16)?

_____

_____

_____

_____

_____

The psalmist hopes that God will fulfill all the plans and petitions of the king (Psa 20:4–5). How do you understand the psalmist's hope that God will give the king "your heart's desire" (20:4)? Would it benefit you if God granted you all your desires? Why or why not? Why would the psalmist want this for the king? What steps can you take to ensure that your desires align with God's?

_____

_____

_____

The psalmist asserts his trust in God and contrasts it with trusting in military strength (20:6–8). Note his confidence in God's help ("he will answer him," 20:6). How confident are you in God's help? What kinds of things beside God do you put your trust in? How can you remind yourself not to trust in "chariots" or "horses"?

_____

_____

_____

For other royal psalms, read Psalms 2, 45, 72 and 132. What do these psalms say about the reign of God? What are some ways that you can recognize God's sovereignty in your life?

_____

_____

_____

THE KING OF GLORY COMES IN

Pray that God would fill you with a sense of His presence.

Read Psalm 24.

Psalm 24 is a temple entry psalm that spells out the requirements for entering God's temple. What are these requirements (24:3–4)? What does it mean to have "clean hands and a pure heart"?

_____

_____

Would you describe yourself as clean and pure? What actions can you take to ensure that you align with this description?

_____

_____

The psalmist begins by pointing out that the entire world belongs to the Lord (24:1–2). Given this, why does the psalm emphasize going to the temple? What is the relationship between ascending the "hill of the Lord" and seeking the face of God (24:3, 6)?

_____

_____

How has Christ's work as the "great high priest" made it possible for us to enter into God's presence (see Heb 9:11–14)?

_____

_____

Psalm 24:7-10 describes a procession where God's presence—most likely symbolized by the ark of the covenant—enters the temple. The ark was a golden chest that represented God's throne (Exod 25:10-22). How does the psalmist describe God in Psalm 24:7-10? What was the effect for the ancient Israelites of seeing a representation of God's presence entering the temple?

_____

_____

_____

How do you experience God's presence in your life?

_____

_____

_____

As believers today, we are described as God's temple with the Holy Spirit dwelling in us (see 1 Cor 3:16-17). How does this influence the way you read this psalm? How does this awareness affect the way you read the requirements of temple entry (Psa 24:4)?

_____

_____

_____

For other temple entry psalms, read Psalms 15, 26, 101 and 118. What do these psalms say about the presence of God? If we hope to be in God's presence, how should we act? In light of Christ's presence in believers (Gal 2:20), what steps can you take today to acknowledge God's presence?

_____

_____

_____

GIVE THANKS TO THE LORD

Pray that God would give you a spirit of thanksgiving toward Him.

Read Psalm 92.

Psalm 92 is a thanksgiving psalm. This type of psalm would have led a congregation of worshipers in giving thanks. The psalmist emphasizes the value of giving thanks to God. How does the psalmist do so (92:2–3)?

_____

_____

_____

How do you give thanks to God? How often do you thank Him?

_____

_____

The psalmist praises God for His great works in 92:4–5. What type of works do you think he had in mind? What works do you praise God for?

_____

_____

_____

Are you made glad by God's works? How do you express this gladness?

_____

_____

_____

The psalmist describes those who do not understand God's works in 92:6–9. What words does he use to describe them? Why do these people fail to understand God's works? How does the psalmist contrast these people with the righteous (92:12–14)?

_____

_____

_____

Compare Jesus' statements about who is "blessed" in Matthew 5:3–12. For what purpose does the psalmist say the righteous flourish (Psa 92:15)? How do the attributes of God described in Psalm 92:15 encourage thanksgiving?

_____

_____

_____

For other thanksgiving psalms, read Psalms 30, 34, 107 and 138. What do these psalms give thanks for? How do they encourage you to express your thankfulness to God?

_____

_____

_____

CONCLUSION

God wants to hear from His people, whether we are joyful or sad, confident or shaken, thankful or despairing. The ancient Israelites praised God and boldly cried out to Him, but you have an even greater guarantee that He will hear you, in Christ's sacrifice and mediating work (1 Tim 2:5; Heb 8:6). You can also approach God confidently because Jesus, who was tempted and tried just like you, sympathizes with your weaknesses (see Heb 4:14–16). So cry out to Him. And may you have confidence that He will hear you, whether your heart is overflowing with praise or overcome with grief. May you bring all things to Him.

PART II

WORSHIPING AN EVER-PRESENT GOD

The psalms most familiar to us are often those that speak to our experience of wrestling the chaos in and around us. They are psalms that reach out to the God of all comfort when we face trials, suffering and sin. In spite of the gulf between our lives and those of the psalmists, their words still resonate with us today, speaking of the universality of our need for God. Among the 150 psalms, there is at least one for almost any situation—from the hope the psalmist offers in Psalm 91 to the regret of sin expressed in Psalm 51.

In Part I, we looked at eight different types of psalms. We saw expressions of authentic worship as the psalmists voiced grief and fear along with praise and thanksgiving. We learned that God wants to hear from us, whether our hearts are filled with joy or heavy with sorrow.

The psalms that bring us such comfort seem so intensely personal that at times we may forget they were originally sung or recited in public. Their purpose is not merely to bring comfort to the individual, but to allow the individual to proclaim God's comfort to others. In the next eight lessons, we'll look at eight well-known psalms. We'll examine what they teach us about God and what they reveal about His great love and concern for us.

THE BLESSED PERSON

Pray that God would help you love His Word.

Read Psalm 1.

It's comforting to read that God will bless His people. In Psalm 1, a wisdom psalm, we find the means for the blessing as the psalmist contrasts the way of the righteous and the way of the wicked. The psalm begins by praising the person who avoids sinful ways and delights in God's law, calling such a person "blessed."

In Psalm 1:1, the psalmist says there are three things we should avoid: "counsel," "way" and "seat." What do these different areas emphasize, and why should we avoid them?

_____

_____

_____

What is the distinction between the wicked, the sinners, and the scoffers? What is the importance of this distinction for us today?

_____

_____

_____

Instead of associating with the wicked person, the "blessed" person delights in God's law. The word usually translated "meditate" in Psalm 1:2 literally means "to murmur" or "to read out loud." Do you regularly read God's Word out loud? What are some benefits of doing so?

_____

_____

Read Joshua 1:8. What does it say is the purpose of "meditating" on God's Word?

_____

_____

_____

Psalm 1:3–4 contrasts the security of the righteous and the wicked. "Chaff" refers to the stalks of wheat that the wind would blow away during the winnowing process. How does this description fit the wicked?

_____

_____

_____

In what ways is the righteous one compared to a tree? How does delighting in God's law give you the stability described in Psalm 1:3 (compare Jer 17:7–8)?

_____

_____

_____

How do the analogies in Psalm 1:3–4 relate to God's judgment in Psalm 1:5?

_____

_____

The final verse of the psalm asserts that the LORD "knows" the ways of the righteous and the wicked. What does it mean that God knows your ways (compare Psa 31:7)? How does God's knowledge of our ways relate to Jesus' teaching about not acting to garner praise from others (Matt 6:1–18)?

_____

_____

_____

THE INESCAPABLE PRESENCE OF GOD

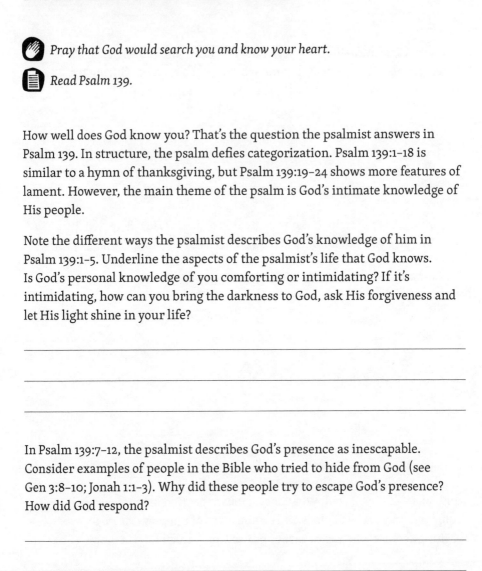

Pray that God would search you and know your heart.

Read Psalm 139.

How well does God know you? That's the question the psalmist answers in Psalm 139. In structure, the psalm defies categorization. Psalm 139:1–18 is similar to a hymn of thanksgiving, but Psalm 139:19–24 shows more features of lament. However, the main theme of the psalm is God's intimate knowledge of His people.

Note the different ways the psalmist describes God's knowledge of him in Psalm 139:1–5. Underline the aspects of the psalmist's life that God knows. Is God's personal knowledge of you comforting or intimidating? If it's intimidating, how can you bring the darkness to God, ask His forgiveness and let His light shine in your life?

In Psalm 139:7–12, the psalmist describes God's presence as inescapable. Consider examples of people in the Bible who tried to hide from God (see Gen 3:8–10; Jonah 1:1–3). Why did these people try to escape God's presence? How did God respond?

Have there been times in your life when you wished you could hide from God? How should you bring all of your life to Him (as we discussed in Part I)?

_____

_____

_____

The psalmist praises God for being personally involved in His creation (Psa 139:13–16). God's knowledge of the psalmist stretches from before his conception to future events (139:16). What does this knowledge say about God's purpose for each of us (read Jer 1:5)? Note how the psalmist responds to God's intimate involvement in his life (Psa 139:17–18).

_____

_____

_____

Psalm 139:19–22 shifts the focus to the wicked. The psalmist aligns himself with God by counting those who hate God as enemies. How do you respond to people who speak against God "with malicious intent" (139:20)? How does your life align with God's will for it, and how do you reflect Him?

_____

_____

_____

The psalmist closes by inviting God to examine him for any offensive ways (139:24). Do you intentionally invite God to examine your heart like this? Write down a list of the things that God reveals to you and pray about them.

_____

_____

_____

_____

A BROKEN AND CONTRITE HEART

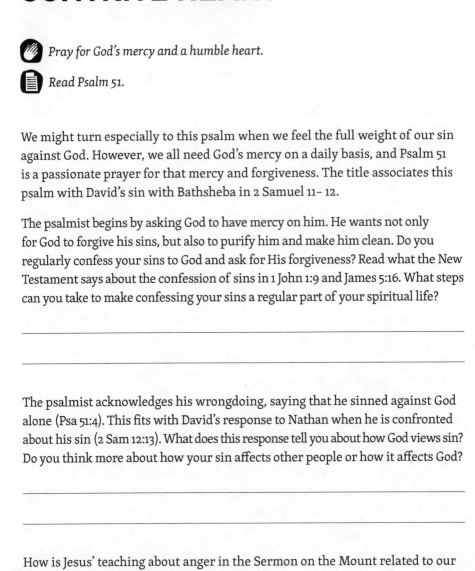 *Pray for God's mercy and a humble heart.*

Read Psalm 51.

We might turn especially to this psalm when we feel the full weight of our sin against God. However, we all need God's mercy on a daily basis, and Psalm 51 is a passionate prayer for that mercy and forgiveness. The title associates this psalm with David's sin with Bathsheba in 2 Samuel 11– 12.

The psalmist begins by asking God to have mercy on him. He wants not only for God to forgive his sins, but also to purify him and make him clean. Do you regularly confess your sins to God and ask for His forgiveness? Read what the New Testament says about the confession of sins in 1 John 1:9 and James 5:16. What steps can you take to make confessing your sins a regular part of your spiritual life?

_____

_____

The psalmist acknowledges his wrongdoing, saying that he sinned against God alone (Psa 51:4). This fits with David's response to Nathan when he is confronted about his sin (2 Sam 12:13). What does this response tell you about how God views sin? Do you think more about how your sin affects other people or how it affects God?

_____

_____

How is Jesus' teaching about anger in the Sermon on the Mount related to our sin against God and others (see Matt 5:21–26)?

_____

_____

In Psalm 51:7–12, the psalmist pleads for cleansing and restoration. He asks God not to take away His presence. How does that request compare with Psalm 139:7–12 (see also 1 Sam 16:14)? What led God to remove His Spirit from Saul? How can we be confident that God will not remove His presence from us (compare 1 John 4:13–16)?

_____

_____

_____

_____

The psalmist does not ask for mercy for his sake alone. He plans to use God's forgiveness in his life to teach others of God's great mercy (Psa 51:13–15). Do you keep your forgiveness hidden from others? How can you use the forgiveness God has extended to you to teach others about His character and salvation?

_____

_____

_____

According to Psalm 51:16–17, what kind of sacrifices does God desire? What does it mean to have a "broken spirit"?

_____

_____

_____

Would you describe your heart as "broken and contrite"? How do the sacrifices of God in Psalm 51:17 compare with Paul's instructions to present ourselves as a "living sacrifice" (see Rom 12:1–2)?

_____

_____

_____

TAKING REFUGE IN GOD

Pray that the Lord would be your dwelling place.

Read Psalm 91.

The image of God as our refuge and fortress is comforting in times of trouble. Psalm 91, a psalm of confidence that emphasizes God's protection, opens by affirming the safety we enjoy in His shelter. The psalmist uses two names for God: the Most High and the Almighty. What do these names emphasize about the nature of God?

_____

_____

_____

How do these names highlight God's ability to protect His people? How is this particularly comforting to you?

_____

_____

_____

The dangers described in Psalm 91:3–6 are things we cannot anticipate— diseases and traps—that can strike at any time. What are some unexpected dangers you have faced in your life? Were you able to rely on God as your refuge and fortress? We can always turn to Him in times of trouble (see also Rom 5:1–5; 1 Pet 1:3–5).

_____

_____

_____

_____

Psalm 91:7 describes a chaotic battle where thousands are dying. However, those who take refuge in the Most High do not need to fear. The psalmist promises that no evil or plague will affect these people (Psa 91:10). How should you understand this in light of the many verses that promise the righteous will suffer (compare 2 Cor 1:5; Phil 1:29; 1 Pet 4:12–19)?

_____

_____

_____

The psalmist discusses God's angels in Psalm 91:11–12. They guard and protect God's people even against small accidents (like striking your foot on a stone). Read Matthew 4:6–7. How did Satan distort this passage about angels when he tempted Jesus in the wilderness? How did Jesus respond?

_____

_____

_____

Psalm 91 concludes with God Himself affirming that He will deliver and protect those who know His name. He promises to answer those who call on Him. Read 1 Kings 18:26–29. How does God's promise here compare with the response the prophets of Baal received when calling upon their god? Reflect on the knowledge that God personally promises to answer you.

_____

_____

_____

LESSON 5

UNDERSTANDING THE PROSPERITY OF THE WICKED

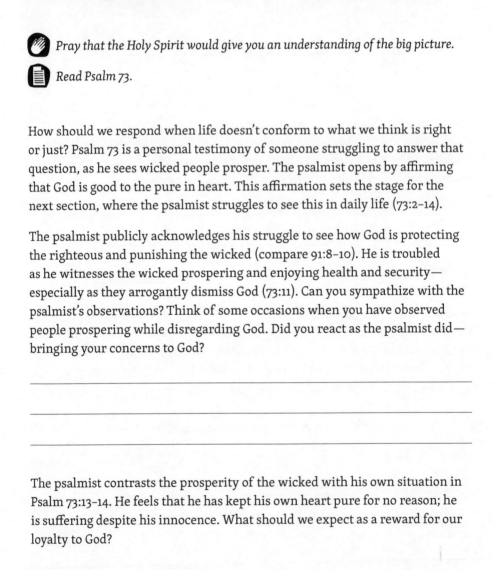 Pray that the Holy Spirit would give you an understanding of the big picture.

Read Psalm 73.

How should we respond when life doesn't conform to what we think is right or just? Psalm 73 is a personal testimony of someone struggling to answer that question, as he sees wicked people prosper. The psalmist opens by affirming that God is good to the pure in heart. This affirmation sets the stage for the next section, where the psalmist struggles to see this in daily life (73:2–14).

The psalmist publicly acknowledges his struggle to see how God is protecting the righteous and punishing the wicked (compare 91:8–10). He is troubled as he witnesses the wicked prospering and enjoying health and security—especially as they arrogantly dismiss God (73:11). Can you sympathize with the psalmist's observations? Think of some occasions when you have observed people prospering while disregarding God. Did you react as the psalmist did—bringing your concerns to God?

_____

_____

_____

The psalmist contrasts the prosperity of the wicked with his own situation in Psalm 73:13–14. He feels that he has kept his own heart pure for no reason; he is suffering despite his innocence. What should we expect as a reward for our loyalty to God?

_____

_____

_____

Does the promise that God is good to those who are pure in heart mean that they will not suffer (see Phil 3:8–11; Col 1:24; 1 Pet 2:19; 3:14–18)? Think of biblical examples of people who suffered despite their faith in God.

_____

_____

_____

What is the turning point for the psalmist (see Psa 73:15– 17)? Why do you think going to the sanctuary of God (i.e., the temple) changes the psalmist's focus? How does it give him an understanding of the big picture?

_____

_____

_____

In ancient Israel, the temple represented God's presence. How do you enter God's presence today? How does it help you envision God's perspective?

_____

_____

_____

Contrast the psalmist's description of the wicked in Psalm 73:18–20 with 73:4–12. What accounts for the difference? Contrast the psalmist's description of himself in 73:21–26 and 73:13–14. How does understanding the big picture help you trust God?

_____

_____

_____

THE LORD IS YOUR KEEPER

Pray that the Lord will keep you from harm.

Read Psalm 121.

As believers, we enjoy the protection of the Creator of heaven and earth. This protection is beautifully portrayed in Psalm 121—a psalm of confidence and one of the "Songs of Ascents" (Pss 120–134). This title most likely refers to an "ascent" made by pilgrims to Jerusalem to worship. These psalms frequently mention Jerusalem and Zion; they also refer to the temple.

The psalmist begins by lifting his eyes to the hills. The hills may represent hidden dangers, foreign gods that were often worshiped from hills (see Jer 3:23), the natural protection hills provided (Psa 125:2), or God Himself coming down from on high to protect His people. The first option emphasizes the need for help. The second option contrasts idols—which provide no help—with God. The third option contrasts earthly security with God's help. The fourth option is a call for God to act. The psalmist's question, "From where does my help come?" refers to the object of his trust and security. Where do you find your trust and security in life? Other than God, what do you place your trust in?

_____

_____

_____

The places where we experience fear and anxiety might suggest what our modern idols are. How can you pray for God's help in these areas? How can your community assist you in this?

_____

_____

_____

_____

When the psalmist asserts that his help comes from the LORD, he mentions God's creation of heaven and earth. How does God's role as Creator make Him more qualified to be our help? Read Colossians 1:15–20. How does the preeminence of Christ over creation make Him qualified to be our Savior?

_____

_____

_____

Much of Psalm 121 is a description of the constant protection of God. How does the psalmist describe the protection God provides? What does it mean that God is your "keeper"? Can you think of an instance where God "kept" you from something harmful?

_____

_____

_____

The psalmist stresses that God's protection is with us always—whether day or night, God does not sleep. Which of the attributes of God described in this psalm bring you comfort, and why?

_____

_____

_____

FORSAKEN BY GOD

Pray that God would give you a new appreciation for Christ's sacrifice.

Read Psalm 22.

We can't escape this life without experiencing trials. The Psalms show us that crying out to God during our trials is acceptable and appropriate. Psalm 22 is a lament psalm best known for its opening line, quoted by Jesus as He suffered on the cross (see Matt 27:46; Mark 15:34). There are several other connections between this psalm and the Gospel accounts of Christ's death. (Compare Psa 22:7 with Matt 27:39 and Mark 15:29; Psa 22:8 with Matt 27:43; Psa 22:18 with Matt 27:35, Mark 15:24 and Luke 23:34). What do these connections teach us about how God's plan of salvation is presented throughout Scripture?

How does Psalm 22 help you understand Christ's suffering on the cross? How does reflecting on Christ's suffering encourage you in your trials?

_____

_____

_____

In its original context, Psalm 22 expressed the extreme anguish and suffering of the psalmist. Through all the physical suffering he describes (see Psa 22:14–18), he is most troubled by his feeling that God is absent. God has helped people in the past (Psa 22:4–5), and the psalmist has been faithful from birth (Psa 22:9–10), but God is not answering his cries (Psa 22:2, 7–8). Have you experienced a time in your life when you felt like God was absent or not answering you? Looking back on the situation, can you see God's presence?

_____

_____

_____

_____

Despite God's apparent absence, the psalmist continues to call out to Him (Psa 22:19–21). Read Luke 18:1–8. What does that parable teach about persistent prayer? How do you remind yourself to be faithful in prayer when it seems God isn't responding?

_____

_____

_____

The second half of Psalm 22 dramatically turns from lament to praise (Psa 22:22–31). The psalmist responds to God's salvation by praising the LORD among his own people, all the peoples of the earth, and even future generations. How have you responded to God's salvation? How can you proclaim what God has done for you to others?

_____

_____

_____

THE GOOD SHEPHERD

Pray that God would lead you in the path of righteousness.

Read Psalm 23.

Psalm 23 may be the best known passage in the Bible. The psalm depicts God as a shepherd who shows His concern for us. How does the "shepherd" lead the psalmist in Psalm 23:2–3? Read John 10:11–18. What are the characteristics of the "Good Shepherd" there?

_____

_____

_____

The "valley of the shadow of death" contrasts with the "green pastures" and "still waters." Are you more likely to recognize God's hand in your life when traveling through "green pastures" or the "valley of the shadow of death"? What can you do to recognize God's guiding presence in all aspects of your life?

_____

_____

_____

The psalmist says God's rod and staff comfort him. A shepherd would use a rod or staff to protect and guide his sheep. Can you think of a time when you felt God's discipline guiding you? How is His discipline a sign of His love (see also Psa 94:12; Heb 12:6; Rev 3:19)?

_____

_____

_____

The psalm reveals the purpose for God's protection of His people: "for His name's sake" (Psa 23:3) How does God's protection serve this purpose? What can you do to ensure the name of God is upheld?

_____

_____

_____

The psalmist shifts from the imagery of a shepherd leading his sheep to the imagery of a host serving his guest (Psa 23:5). In the ancient Near East, hosts were responsible for their guests' safety. Here the psalmist describes his enjoyment of a peaceful feast, while being surrounded by his enemies. How is the image of a host similar to the image of the shepherd? Which of these images do you relate to more?

_____

_____

_____

How have you seen God guiding, protecting or nourishing you—even in times of difficulty?

_____

_____

_____

CONCLUSION

Our favorite psalms tend to be those that reveal God's great care for His people, likely because they teach us that God will be with us—guiding us through both times of joy and trial. He is there when we sin or fall away, ready to demonstrate His great mercy and forgiveness. He is present during our struggles, even when we cannot feel His presence. However, God's love for us is not for our sake alone. He shows us mercy and guides us "for His name's sake" (Psa 23:3). He works in our lives so that we will tell others what He has done for us (Psa 22:22–31), and so that we may have a deeper relationship with Him. May you feel God's intimate love—perfectly expressed by the sending of His Son (Eph 2:4–5)—and respond by telling others about His work.